Strength
Within
Tears

Strength Within Tears

Within

Tears

A Path To Crying

By Shane E. DeMorais

iUniverse, Inc.
Bloomington

Strength Within Tears
A Path To Crying

Company and product names mentioned herein are the trademarks or registered trademarks of their respective owners

iUniverse books may be ordered through booksellers or by contacting:

iUniverse
1663 Liberty Drive
Bloomington, IN 47403
www.iuniverse.com
1-800-Authors (1-800-288-4677)

Because of the dynamic nature of the Internet, any web addresses or links contained in this book may have changed since publication and may no longer be valid. The views expressed in this work are solely those of the author and do not necessarily reflect the views of the publisher, and the publisher hereby disclaims any responsibility for them.

Any people depicted in stock imagery provided by Thinkstock are models, and such images are being used for illustrative purposes only.
Certain stock imagery © Thinkstock.

ISBN: 978-1-4697-8151-8 (sc)
ISBN: 978-1-4697-8152-5 (ebk)

Printed in the United States of America

iUniverse rev. date: 02 / 21 / 2012

This book is dedicated to all those who chose to move from their minds into their hearts. Do not ignore the journey and only focus on the destination, for the journey is where the magic happens.

CONTENTS

DISCLAIMER

Contained in this book are step-by-step instructions for a technique that will, hopefully, result in you remembering how to cry, culminating in an ability to let go and release pain that you have kept in. Both men and women can use the technique. However, myself being a man, it is a more masculine approach to remembering something I'd forgotten long ago.

Please note that I am *not* a trained professional in any sense of the word at the time of writing this book. Not in any of the modern psychological, psychiatrical, or sociological fields. I am not a spiritual teacher, nor a certified healer of any sort.

Please consult your physician, or practicing counselor
before beginning this process.

INTRODUCTION

"The only journey is the one within"
—Rainer Maria Rilke

For most of my adult life I have never properly grieved. In retrospect I understand what transpired in my youth to cause me to withhold my tears. It wasn't due to fear, or abuse, or a strict upbringing, my decision to never cry again was partly due to my environment growing up in London, England and how I was building up my Ego (and forging my Shadow). Many years have past since that day and although I have pursued a career as a Software Engineer my life has given me many opportunities to move away from championing an identity and embracing the power of spirit, all of which was born out of a strong desire for personal growth in order to find my true path. A path that brings forth experiences of truly felt love for myself and my fellow Human Beings.

Seeking that feeling has always been my goal; I cannot remember a time where I didn't want to follow my heart. I do not accept the fact that I have to follow the established rule of not doing such a thing. With that overriding purpose I can now say that my life has been blessed and guided, but not always easy. Still, when I look back I catch glimpses of signposts for roads I have taken, and of those I didn't heed which somehow manage to end up before me once more begging to be seen. I have learned to spot those missed opportunities, and with guidance managed to steer into them. The lessons on how to trust my intuition by repeatedly dropping from within my head down into my heart, by embracing the silence that grows into peace and tranquility, continue to present themselves, and they are oh so welcomed.

When yielding to my inner feelings, and walking several steps in another new direction, I'd contemplate my choice; why the smooth tarmac, or why the gobble stones which constantly manage to trip me up with every step? Sometimes the answers come immediately, other times I know that I have to be patient, let time move on before understanding. Of all these roads leading forwards in career, family, and romance, I have found that I have grown the most when I have mustered the courage to travel ones of romance. Of course during those times it felt like gloriously smooth tarmac to begin with and ending with huge mountains of stones requiring all my strength to conquer.

Thankfully I have been fortunate to embarked on a few of these roads of romance, always unwary of the outcome, unsure of where it will lead, completely lost in the excitement of a new opportunity for giving and receiving love and affection. Now I can only but smile at the man I was, and hold reverence for the man I am becoming. The pinnacle to date of these treks has given rise to a realization that a vital element for releasing pain had been left behind somewhere in my past many years ago, the tool of crying.

As I entered my midlife accepting my vulnerability, but not recognizing that I was intensely attached to the idea of receiving affection and afraid of abandonment, I dove once more into the realm of love. As time passed my love for this woman grew. However, where I thought the relationship was going was not where it was going. Very quickly I found myself feeling that which I feared the most; being abandoned. I found myself leaving the domain of my heart and securely locking myself in the trap of Mind. My ego was winning the battle of my spiritual quest. My behavior was selfish and immature. I attempted to win back the blanket of affection with words that were strong in presentation and argument, yet my actions were weak in love and acceptance. I lost my power of Self, and slid into egoic antics. May I point out that getting angry at someone while trying to convince them that they should return your love is a rather foolish way to proceed, anger pushes people away as anyone on the receiving end can attest to.

I am grateful for my meditative practice as it yielded an ability to witness myself while embroiled in a battle with my ego. I became aware that my behavior was not in line with how I wanted to live my life. It was destructive in that my need for affection, which wasn't being met, was causing stress to accumulate as I wasn't releasing the pain in my heart. I was confronted with a choice, lose myself in my mind or find a way to empty my heart of the grief I was feeling. This book is a testament as to how I responded. I found strength within my tears.

The gift of crying we humans possess can never be overstated in its importance, and to arrive at a place unable to properly grieve when the relationship was ending caused me to make the decision that will affect me for the rest of my life. My decision to stop running from my grief, to stop denying that it wouldn't affect me, and to find a way to make myself cry in order to squeeze as many drops of pain from my heart as possible was paramount to my survival. What transpired over that short period of time was for me quite astonishing, deeply felt insecurities were realized and a more grounded person emerged. I also found that I had a burning desire to share what I had done.

WHY A BOOK?

I wrote this book because I found myself frustrated when people (or books) would prescribe dealing with pain by starting with the statement, "*Go into the pain*", followed by a set of instructions that required an understanding of that statement. That just didn't work for me because I really needed someone to explain how to go into the pain, or at least guide me to a place where I could see that I was blocking myself from understanding how. Incredibly once I had discovered how to cry again and was relaying my remembered skill to a friend, I too found myself using that same phrase, several times in fact. Resulting in my friend screaming out in his own frustration "*Stop saying that!! It's not helping!*" To which I began to think that perhaps I wasn't the only one who didn't understand what people meant either.

So now over the course of this book I present the Basic Ingredients (mechanics) of the technique concluding in the complete technique as step-step instructions for you to use, followed by Personal Insights gained during my evolvement as a man that were necessary in order to be free to cry.

I've chosen to split the information in two parts simply because to present a step-step procedure on how I induced myself to cry would have been rather confusing for you. If one has reached a point in life where they find themselves unable to cry, having a recipe wouldn't help much. We're not building a car. Like cooking, there are ingredients beyond the physical that are necessary to produce the desired result. Cooking without love will yield a nutritious meal, but the eater will not remember the experience, nor will they fully relish the food. The same principles apply here. I had to gain profound understandings of my nature, where I was misunderstanding life's lessons and how to correct my course. With that in mind it seemed natural that I would have to erect signposts for you, the reader, so that when you are ready to cry you will understand what will be required of you. Those signposts appear in the Personal Insights section. They are invaluable to me, and everyday I have to remind myself of them in order to keep moving forward on my journey of growth and self-discovery.

BASIC INGREDIENTS

"The only real stumbling block is fear of failure. In cooking you've got to have a what-the-hell attitude."
—Julia Child

As with any recipe there are the basic ingredients, the how-to steps, and things to look out for while you execute. Naturally then I will be guiding you on what you will need, as well as explain why they are needed. I'll introduce concepts such as the Cave, giving oneself permission, as well as emphasize the need for courage, and in keeping an open mind. All these things separately are useful tools for everyday life, bringing them together with a firm intention provides a strong foundation for healing as well as a sense that you are ready and can take on a what-the-hell attitude towards your path of growth.

THE CAVE

The most obvious first ingredient is a place where you will go to cry. I call it a "Cave". It is a place where I could go and be in solitude, a room where I created a comfort zone in which I was able to surrender to the deeply felt vulnerability that crying creates. I'd dim the lights, sit on a couch, occasionally pulling my knees up against my chest to feel a little more secure, a little safer, and await the moment when the tears would begin to fall.

The concept of a cave may be familiar to some of you. Perhaps you may not have access to a cave, that's understandable, however it is important that you acquire your own space to be alone. Asking a friend for use of their space may work, just get creative if you have to. Now remember that while in the space you have to feel safe, so simply parking your car somewhere may not be the best solution.

PERMISSION

This is the single, most powerful ingredient I bring to my Cave.

Marcia Kimmel, an acting coach in San Francisco, told me to "*give myself permission*" to feel awkward when I was doing an improvisational exercise, and it really helped overcome the self-consciousness of the moment. Well, naturally, crying was something that I always felt uncomfortable doing, and after a while I realized that giving myself permission was the most invaluable tool that, as an adult, I really needed when attempting something outside of my comfort zone. I gave myself permission to let go, permission to loosen the guards around my heart, permission to feel a sense of softening in order to move closer to crying.

This simple visualization technique may help you overcome the inability to give yourself permission. I'm using a rose due to it's archetypal nature as a symbol of one's Self. Visualize a gold rose; this is a rose of permission. Present it to yourself and express in your own language what you are giving yourself permission for. Visualize the rose leaving your hand and entering your body. Allow yourself to breath in this permission, recognize what the effect is when you realize that perhaps due to influences over you as a child you had been unable to accept that you could override the feelings of not being allowed to move in your own direction.

To reinforce this permission you can use an affirmation. Affirmations are powerful tools to keep oneself focused. Here is a Permission affirmation...

> *"I give myself permission to let go of my struggles, fears, and heartaches. I give myself permission to let go of my pain."*

You may wish to memorize it and recite it before, during, and after your session.

AN OPEN MIND

One who has forgotten how to cry should realize that the body will remember when the mind is quiet and open to the experience. While going through the process my ego would continually knock on my door, so whenever I felt my mind pulling me out of my heart space I'd say the "*Permission*" affirmation. Then continue.

Give yourself permission to leave all judgments outside the Cave.

During the process I'd recommend you make friends with your ego, and let it know that for a short period of time it's free to go on vacation. Visualize taking it to the airport and giving it a return ticket, helping it get on a plane. Then before you exit the Cave, visualize yourself picking up your ego at the airport, welcoming it back. This might sound strange, yet the mind is a strange beast, and something as weird as this actually does work to some extent. Remember to be open to new concepts.

COURAGE

It took courage to admit to myself that I needed to find a way to release my pain in a non-aggressive manner. What I was about to do I recognized as long overdue, and again I had to muster my courage. In your case I'm sure it took courage to search for a self-help book that would assist you in this, and courage to purchase it. It will take courage to gather the necessary items and secure the cave, courage to get permission to be alone and away from other people in the house if necessary.

Remind yourself of these things. The courage needed you have within you. Time to bring it forth.

A GROUNDING TECHNIQUE

We've all had the experience of not keeping a train of thought, having our minds constantly flicker one way then the next, zoning out while driving, or riding public transportation. Grounding is simply a way to bring oneself into the present moment, quieting the mind and becoming still

Here is a simple grounding technique:

> Sitting with your back straight, visualize a rope dropping down from the base of your spine to the center of the earth. When it reaches the center imagine it being secured to the core and becoming taut, anchoring you and pulling you a little towards the ground.

> Now visual a large beach ball above your head. This ball becomes filled with the golden light of unconditional love. Once it's filled, reach up and pierce the bottom causing all of that golden light to pour out over you and into you.

> Hold the image of you being anchored and covered in golden light for a few moments, breathing deeply. Let go of any other thoughts and allow yourself to become very much in the present moment.

MUSIC

Kurt Vonnegut once stated "*Music is to me, proof of the existence of God.*" I'd have to agree. I have not found any other creative form that has the ability to move me in ways that music has. So it seemed natural that in my quest to release my pain I would require an avenue that would stir my soul, taking me to a place where I could delve into my heart and let the flood gates open.

I chose music that would take me deep, which would stir the very core of my being. Music that I knew would, if I allowed it, cause my eyes to well up with tears.

I knew that I probably wasn't going to cry if I heard myself crying, as that was one of the triggers that held me back in the past. I needed to let go of all judgment. Listening to the music in headphones at a volume that drowned out the sound I was making really helped me stay focused on maintaining a quiet mind. When I did find myself judging I would simply turn deeper into the music.

It's best if you create a playlist for an MP3 player, or burn a CD. Whichever works for you. The first track should be a soft 3-5 minute instrumental song that will be playing during the grounding step.

I have found that the playlist changed because I could cry more easily with some songs, whereas other songs were great for bringing me closer to my heart. I moved tracks around due to the fact that I needed to allow myself time to clear my mind and open my heart, at least for the first few days where I was using this technique.

WARNING: Be advised that the listening to music at loud volumes can cause hearing damage, what I'm prescribing is setting the volume just loud enough and within a safe limit below the threshold of damaging your hearing.

A PILLOW

As I went deeper into my heart I found slight resistance here and there. Having a pillow handy allowed me to push my fists into it, tensing and releasing my entire body and giving the restricting emotions an outlet.

I also noticed that I could bury my face into it, and cry much harder. Something I remember doing as a child.

A BLANKET

Not only did a blanket provide me with warmth, it also felt comforting wrapped around my body. It is also another article that I could grip and hold tightly at certain moments. At times, it was available to pull over my head and darken the space even more. For me, having that sense of darkness around was comforting.

A SMALL TOWEL

It's important to me to be comfortable shedding tears, and knowing that I had a towel handy to dry my nose, or wipe away the tears helped. Sometimes I found myself squeezing the towel instead of using the pillow. Another way to let out some of the pain was by holding the towel to my forehead and rubbing my brow.

STEPS FOR CRYING

"An ounce of action is worth a ton of theory."
—Ralph Waldo Emerson

When you're ready to begin the process I would recommend reading this section a few times so as to become familiar with what it all entails. You may choose to visualize going through the entire process, including the crying. This will help you prepare and be more relaxed in continuing.

I advocate setting a time and location in which to let go your tears, keeping to a schedule for a period of two weeks. Having a sense of purpose towards your healing will allow your subconscious to begin preparing for each session and it will also require you to keep the commitment to yourself.

REQUIRED ITEMS

Now that I have outlined the basic ingredients, it's time to gather them. Here's the list.

An Open Mind
Permission
Courage
A "Cave".
Pillow.
Small Towel.
Blanket—Heavy enough so you feel it over your shoulders.
Music.
Headphones.
Music playing device.
A light that can be dimmed, or a small candle safely housed.

NOT REQUIRED (LEAVE 'EM OUT)

Judgment

Self Doubt

Fear (leave a little out each time)

TIME TO CRY

Secure your cave.   Initially you may only need 10-20 minutes.

Alert any other people in the house of your schedule so that people know you will be out of communication for a period of time, and/or will vacate the room for you to use. Making up a story as to what you're doing is fine, however the more honest you are with your intentions the better you'll be able to move towards a more authentic you. If you feel the need to share with others, that's great. Just make sure they know enough to give you space and allow the time to pass without disturbing you.

Gather the items.

Before entering the Cave, you may wish to go through the visualization of sending your ego on a trip.

Recite the Permission affirmation.

I'd ask that you to leave fear outside the Cave, but let's face it, that's a tall order. Best to give yourself permission to feel fear. Then if it arises, acknowledge it verbally (*"hello my fear"*), then clear your mind and focus back in towards the music.

Send your ego on a vacation

Enter the Cave. Lock the door if necessary.

Adjust the heating as needed, as you may choose to keep the blanket over you.

Place the blanket over the couch, and position it so it will be behind you when you are ready to sit down.

Put the towel where it will be within reach.

Load up the music, checking that the volume is adequate in the headphones (not too loud so as to cause hearing damage). Once the volume is set correctly, reset the music and set the headphones to the side.

If you wear glasses you may find it more comfortable to take them off while you've got the headphones on during the session.

Lower the lights, or use the candle.

WARNING: Be sure to have the candle in an appropriately safe candleholder so that the wax doesn't drip everywhere. Also, be cautious on how big the flame will get. Be safe with the open flame. Do not place it near any free flowing fabrics where the fabric will be in danger of catching alight. Please be extremely careful.

Take a seat.

Take a few deep breaths. Quieting your mind.

Allow your body to relax. Take your time.

Recite the Permission affirmation once more.

Put on the headphones.

Wrap the blanket over your shoulders.

Take hold of the towel.

Take a few more deep breaths. Shake of any earlier events. Relax into your body.

Turn on the music.

Now use your grounding technique. It's very important that you do this, as you will be visualizing energy flowing from your head to your heart soon. Grounding will help keep you in the present moment.

Once done with your grounding, allow yourself to drift into the music.

As you listen notice where your energy is. If you are contemplating your pain, or having an inner monologue of some kind, note that. However, continue to breath deeply quieting your mind.

Continue letting go of your thoughts. Diving deeper into the music.

If your eyes are open, try closing them now and again.

Determine where your energy is. If it is in your head, visualize a ball of green energy moving slowly from your head down to your throat and then finally resting in your heart. Let the ball of energy begin to fuse with the walls of your heart. Melting them away.

As this happens, the music may lift old memories of pain up from the deepest places of your heart. Let that happen.

Take a deep breath and sigh.

Allow yourself to feel the pain in your heart. Letting it begin to cause the tears to move.

Remind yourself of the fact that you are safely in your Cave.

Painful images may appear from your past, or they may be what's going on now. Acknowledge them, and let them go. Feel your heart while viewing the images.

Within the music you may find parts that touch you more deeply. Begin to focus more on those parts, feel them fully.

After a period of time you should start to notice that the images, music and your heart are all becoming connected. Shifting the pain to the surface.

Here you may start feeling the tears loosen. Let them flow. Give yourself permission to let go and cry a few tears. Notice how it feels, and let go of any judgments.

As you begin to cry gently, you may find that pulling your knees to your chest, and resting your forehead on them is comforting and facilitates crying even deeper.

Let the music carry you still further into your heart, releasing more tears.

Give yourself permission to sob a little. The body will remember, don't resist too much. Pulling back is ok. Just know that you are now on the path to crying, so take a moment, and then continue.

At this time, I have found that visualizing a mentor, or guardian standing over me and wrapping their arms around me to be hugely comforting. It allowed me to feel that I could lean into someone, and let them take the burden of my pain away for a small time.

After a period of time, neither caring if it has been short or long, you'll find a point where you feel that the session is finished. Bring the volume of the music down a bit, and rest. Take a few deep breaths. Sigh a few times. Acknowledge that you kept the commitment to yourself.

When you are ready, take off the headphones. Sit for another few minutes, then say thank you to yourself for having the courage to undertake this task. Thank yourself for seeing it through. Then commit to another time for another session.

I've found that the more I returned to the Cave the first week, the more I was able to let go. I was also becoming aware of what worked for me, and adjusted the practice accordingly. The first time I only cried for about a minute. The next roughly five minutes. By the end of the week I would go for about twenty minutes, with several bouts during that time.

Remember, adjust elements to suit your particular needs as you are responsible for your own comfort.

IS THAT IT?

Yes, actually, and it's all rather simple when you look at just the mechanics. Yet, as I have stated, my personal insights were what were really needed for me to release my pain. So the next sections are just that, my personal insights. They are my interpretations of well-documented concepts; they are merely designed to evoke questions that may perhaps render you to a deeper curiosity about who you are, and why are you here. Which I hope will, when combined with the above ingredients allow you to dive deeper into your pain and let it go.

PERSONAL INSIGHTS

"Life is the sum of all your choices."

—Albert Camus

All of us have a story, each person's is just as important as the next. My story, my life experience up to now has led to these pages. I will not outline my life here, not in an autobiographical manner, as I do not believe it will serve you. I chose instead to document my personal insights in order to fulfill that strong desire to share. And in the end they may help you to understand your own life better, and seek further growth, or perhaps they will provide you with another source that confirms your own understandings, or simply shed light on concepts that you too may have found as confusing as I did.

One of the epiphanies I had is that my lack of ability to cry had established a sense that I was only touching the surface of my experiences. Anxiety and stress, accumulated over time, had no real path outwards except through my mind. Yielding even more stress that clearly could have led to a breakdown.

What my technique did was to allow me to release my pain in a healthy manner. I did keep tabs on myself to make sure I didn't sink into a depression. Although with proper guidance from people more skilled in this area, allowing a short bout of depression to take hold may reveal a deeper life purpose for you. Please seek proper counseling if you become aware that you're having difficulty engaging with your life. Lying in bed not looking forward to the day, having an inordinate amount of melancholy may be early indicators.

These days I acknowledge that crying is not a sign of weakness; you may feel this effect either during or after a session, let it go. To know the value of life one must accept that one is a vulnerable creature. In doing so I have found I can now embrace life even more.

At times in my life I feel like I'm being dragged through the muck and when I try to speak up I find my voice fails me. Now we all have something to say, especially to ourselves, and if it's important enough we should be willing to spend the time traveling through the muck to say it. Not allowing ourselves to be vulnerable, to hold back the tears when the pain gets too great, denies us our voice when matters of the heart are at stake. Why travel through all the muck if when the time comes we can't trust in our vulnerability and speak our truth? Whether it's to a loved one, a boss, or a stranger who has wronged us. I'm not referring to exploding in anger. I'm referring to having a calm conversation where we acknowledge whatever is causing us pain.

In doing so, I've found that my authentic self is allowed to emerge. I have become stronger simply because I took ownership of the situation. I owned it for myself, taking responsibility for my part which in turn caused the fear to dissipate as it unfolded. Rest assured I still have my moments where I once again feel afraid of my vulnerability and when that happens I simply remind myself that I have been through the muck, and most certainly will travel through it again and survive because I have a way to release my pain.

> *"To the mind that is still, the whole universe surrenders."*
>
> —Lieh Tzu

COMMITMENT

"Never rely on a second arrow. If you rely on a second arrow you will be careless with the first. Every time you must be convinced that you have only one choice, and that you must hit your target with your one and only arrow."

—Kenko-Khosi

Our life is made up of a series of journeys and when you go through the crying process you will understand that one journey is about to end, the next to start.

Is it worth it to you to travel the remaining part?

Take a moment and contemplate this question. I know you're reading this book, yet still? Is it worth it to you? Until you have a resounding "*YES*", then you will only dip your toe in.

Commitment is paramount, it is the key to growth.

Sometime in my past I made the decision to never cry again. I did it because I didn't want to admit to myself that I was vulnerable. I believe it was around 11 or 12 years old,. I stuck to that decision, making a commitment to myself never to allow my vulnerability to show. I would control it, thereby demonstrating that I had the world licked and that it would never fully break my heart again. That the world may beat me down, but not break me. As a boy about to become a man, a warrior of this world, I would be able to prove how strong I was in the truest of British ways. The stiff upper lip. Boys don't cry! And all that.

Over time I recognized that I wasn't invincible. The amount of energy required to remain stoic was too great. As the years progressed my heart softened. Yet I still held on even tighter for fear of the pain. For fear that if I cracked then everything that I wanted to experience would be lost as I crumbled. The funny thing is that now I realize that by not relaxing into my pain I never fully committed to anything from the deepest place of my heart. I only experienced the world on a superficial level, thinking that I had it all figured out.

Why swim on the surface of life when you can dive in, not with reckless abandon, but with heartfelt Love towards that which is being committed to?

> *"Man was made for Joy and Woe;*
> *And when this we rightly know,*
> *Thro' the World we safely go,*
> *Joy and woe are woven fine,*
> *A clothing for the soul divine."*

—William Blake

PSYCHOLOGY OF CRYING

"When the levee breaks, mamma you gotta move."
—Led Zeppelin

All of us at one time or another in our lives have cried. So why do we cry? Humans are one of the few species to cry due to emotional pain. The action is easy to understand, it's a release. However, how did we develop this release? Does it have benefits, and/or can it be harmful?

Science hasn't really answered these questions simply because it's very difficult to study people crying. Think about it for a moment. My technique requires you to dwell in solitude so that you feel comfortable and safe. If someone were in the space with me, monitoring me, I'd have a very difficult time letting go as ego, self-conscious etc..., play a big part in that. The only information obtained for a study would have to be my own notes on how I felt, what images came into my mind, any resistances that arose. All these would rely on my ability to articulate, to remember and in the end my desire to expose the core of my being to others. I suppose a team could develop a questionnaire, but that's beyond me as to what that would look like. Besides, dealing with pain is a very personal thing, and in the West it requires courage to stand naked offering up ones vulnerability for scrutiny.

In lieu of the above, what I have done is shine a light inwards to see if I can conclude the purpose and benefits of crying for me.

From the age of 1-2 I'd cry due to being in discomfort, and I'm sure most things took me outside my comfort zone since it would be a comfort zone based on my current perception of how my universe worked. That perception being that everybody was in my universe, I was the center of it with everyone serving me.

Some discomfort examples are: Being Hungry. Experiencing bodily pain (stomach ache, diaper rash, teething). Experiencing emotional pain (mother not close, pacifier falling out of my mouth)

These were aspects of my existence that I didn't fully understand. They just happened. I wouldn't call these things elements of fear. I can't imagine I would have the understanding of my vulnerability, therefore why would I be afraid. The crying would stop when the discomfort ended. The discomfort would have to be ended by a guardian—mother, father, grandparent etc… Therefore, it is important to note that I received support during these times.

As my consciousness expanded those discomforts would have also expanded. Bodily pain would now probably include bumping into things, or falling down and sensing people around me become worried, thus the energy in the room shifting and causing me emotional discomfort until a parent/ guardian soothed me.

The crying, as can be observed in most well adjusted children at that age (with well adjusted parents too I might add), comes quickly, lasts for a short period of time, and then is forgotten. As children we have an incredible ability to forgive and forget.

It would seem then that crying at that age had a great deal of benefit to me. Partly due to the release of stress born out of the discomfort, partly due to the fact that I was able to forgive so quickly, and partly due the fact that I received support from another.

Most children are so in the moment, they don't hold onto anything. Their egos, and corresponding shadows, are only beginning to become defined. The Ego being self identity, whereas the Shadow being elements of our personality that we deemed counter-productive to our acceptance in the world, and thus stored away deep. Both may be seen as who we are today and knowing the two sides is important. Shadow work is a new concept and it may prove helpful in unlocking patterns of behavior that will move me closer to my life's purpose.

As I aged, and my ego grew as my understanding of my universe took shape, the ability to forgive began to weaken. Crying bouts lasted longer. I would imagine people that had yanked me out of my comfort zone would've had to work a little harder to earn my forgiveness. Holding a grudge would have been a perceived tool of control. In addition, it was becoming apparent that I wasn't the center of my universe. If I cried, there wasn't a guarantee that someone would be there to comfort and support me, especially when my ability to move around improved substantially. This is an interesting point as it denotes the beginnings of me understanding my vulnerability.

Was crying still healthy for me? I believe to some degree is was. Yet, I was also viewing it as a sign of weakness. Perhaps due to my perceived idea of how a man behaves, which was being constructed while being raised by my mother—an important fact. Lacking guidance to think otherwise the concept of crying started to shift from strengthening me to weakening me. Crying was beginning to be moved into the realm of my Shadow.

I began to cry less and less when in discomfort due to a combination of the "*boys don't cry*" sentiments spoken by adults, and peer pressure. A boy crying would have been ridiculed by his peers, and by older boys. This would have generated feelings of embarrassment, shame and inadequacies. What about someone crossing me, causing a lot of anger and frustration? The inability to choose the avenue of tears would have compounded those feelings causing me to explode and lash out culminating in damage either to myself, or things/ people around me. Of course, being aware, I believed crying was getting me nowhere; it was no longer serving a purpose and had no perceived positive benefits. Concluding in that fateful moment when I decided to shove crying into my Shadow bag completely. I was no longer going to accept my vulnerability, and tears would no longer be used to release the pain as I refused to appear *unmanly*.

The benefits of crying then seemed to be based on how I perceived crying. As I went from baby to young child, young child to boy, boy to man, crying denoted who I was rather than being simply an emotional outlet.

My recent Shadow work made me realize that to be healthier, and have a deeper relationship with myself, with people, and the environment in which I live in, I needed to reclaim crying from my Shadow bag. My perception of crying needed to change. In doing so I reconnected with the positive benefits of crying.

BEING SUPPORTED

An important revelation occurred during the previous exercise of introspection, that is the aspect of feeling supported as influencing my perception of the benefits of crying.

During my crying sessions I had images of people, angels and such, putting their arms around me. Comforting me, supporting me. While documenting the technique I make a point of stating that you too should visualize these images as they proved to be of great benefit to my own healing. Intuitively, I had recognized that I needed to feel supported during the sessions, I must have subconsciously remembered those early years.

Interestingly in my research for writing this book, I came across an article in the Wall St. Journal (May 4th, 2011) entitled *"Read It and Weep, Crybabies."* which stated that people who felt supported during their crying faired much better in deeming crying as beneficial. For those of us on a spiritual path, who have a belief that we are connected to a higher self, supported by that self, this visualization is easier. If you are not on such a path, yet are certainly on a path of growth, it is important to allow yourself to feel supported in anyway you can. Even if it's simply allowing the couch that supports your physical weight, to also support your emotional weight. Giving yourself permission to do so will allow your heart to yield to the idea of receiving support. Over time, the visualizations will take on a different energy. You may find it easier to connect with your surroundings, and those within it, allowing them to nurture you.

COMPASSION

*"If you want others to be happy, practice compassion.
If you want to be happy, practice compassion."*
—Dalai Lama

Compassion can be defined as a sympathetic consciousness of other's distress together with a desire to alleviate it. It literally means to "*suffer with*". Many people understand how to be compassionate towards others. However, during the course of working with the crying technique it's important to have self-compassion. That is, the ability to behave towards yourself as you would another during their suffering. This process of accepting one's vulnerability may be easy for some, difficult for others. If it's difficult for you, admit it. Saying "*This is difficult for me. How would I comfort someone in this situation? How can I apply that to myself?*" Let go of any self-judgments and criticisms. Acknowledge that you are on a path of healing.

These days most people hear "*hey, we're not perfect*". I was fortunate enough to encounter a different point of view. Which is...

The universe is as it is, it does not judge. The mountain doesn't judge the stream that runs through it. You are as you are, the universe isn't judging you either. If it all could be any other way, it would be. Therefore, in this moment the universe and you are perfect.

To render something as imperfect is to first pass judgment on it, to be critical without first just being at one with what is being observed. Attempt to allow your awareness to simply be. The mind still. A good practice I've been using for a while is to pay attention when I look at something. If I catch myself judging, I close my eyes, clear my mind, open my eyes and see without having an inner monologue. Eckhart Tolle advocates such a technique. If you haven't already, I'd recommend reading "*The Power of Now: A Guide to Spiritual Enlightenment*".

If you're waiting to cross the street, or just waiting at a coffee shop for someone, clear your mind and see if you can go for a short period of time without thinking. How does that feel? Let your body relax simply by shifting your attention into your body. Finding a sensation such as aching feet may help draw you in.

Of course, I am always looking for growth in ways that allow me to achieve this state of awareness. To be at peace with myself; to see the true nature of the universe without judging it. To see my own true nature, which is a manifestation of billions of years of evolution, who is Self-aware and able to laugh at the mystery. Yet, it has proven difficult without the ability to accept my vulnerability. Once I was able to do that, I could then appreciate the incredible strength that comes from that acceptance. My first step towards this was in truly diving deep into my tears. Delving inwards. Letting go of my fears.

> "*Internal and external are ultimately one. When you no longer perceive the world as hostile, there is no more fear, and when there is no more fear, you think, speak and act differently. Love and compassion arise, and they affect the world.*"
>
> —Eckhart Tolle

CULTIVATING COMPASSION

Without empathy it will be difficult to move into a more compassionate existence. Empathy is the ability to put yourself in someone else's shoes by imagining in the minutest detail of how it must be to be them in a situation where they are suffering. Recognizing first and foremost that they are simply another human being like you, whilst ignoring the differences of race, color, height, sex as none of it matters at this time. They are suffering, you have suffered. Put yourself in their position for a moment and understand how they feel. How heavy is their heart.

As time goes by you will begin to see yourself in others, and themselves in you. Recognition allows you to honor that person for continuing on despite their struggles, acknowledging the courage in them as well as yourself.

The heart of compassion is desire to alleviate the suffering of the other person. Understanding another person allows you to be a little more forgiving when they may become angry with you, or with someone else. Instead of exploding at them, you'll be able to see through to the truth of the encounter; their suffering. Or if you see someone upset, your empathy may lead you to pause for a moment, still your mind and open your heart offering him or her comfort if possible.

In regards to the person in anger, you may choose to move on, letting their anger flow by you. In doing so you will notice you didn't become burdened with that energy, you didn't have an inner monologue deriding the person for their *inconsiderate* behavior. You were able to allow that person their opportunity to vent in their way, and you yourself were free to continue with your day. If you chose to engage this person in a frank discussion around what the issue is, you may find that by not reacting aggressively, but out of compassion, your calmness will bring the other person into a calmer disposition. Of course, each encounter must be considered for safety before any attempt is made to defuse the situation. Trust your instincts and have a sound exit strategy before engaging any person who may be angry and/or potentially violent.

Reiki has a set of principles that basically are stated as follows:

Just for Today:
I will let go of anger.
I will let go of worry.
I will give thanks for my many blessings.
I will do my work honestly.
I will be kind to my neighbor.

They seem simple enough, yet how many times have I found myself holding on to my anger towards someone? Or steeped in worry about things beyond my control? Have I stopped and looked at my life lately and found things to be grateful for? Have I gone to work accepting that this is the job I chose, and performed my work avoiding the web, email or other such distractions? Did I say hello to people I met on the street?

In order to become a more compassionate person towards others and myself I had to slow down my mind. I had to become more mindful of the present moment. Reminding myself of the Reiki principles every now and again reaffirms my intention towards the goal of compassion. Without which I wouldn't have had the courage, nor desire to find a path to remember how to cry. I wouldn't have had the courage to fall in Love as I wouldn't have had compassion for myself and understood the value of my vulnerability.

Understanding the definition of compassion is the first step. To really know compassion you have to act. Direct your actions towards yourself. One simple exercise can be done first thing in the morning when you see yourself in the mirror. Look into your own eyes. Allow a smile to form. Watch how the eyes take on that smile. Then with authenticity say "*I see you're suffering, this too shall pass*". If you have never done such a thing before; simply looking at yourself, you may find it awkward at first. That's natural. Very rarely are we completely free of our self-conscious self. Notice this, then give yourself permission to feel awkward. Repeat the exercise. Over time you will feel the power of this exercise.

> *Like a beautiful flower, full of color but without scent,*
> *are the fine but fruitless words of him who does not act*
> *accordingly*

> —Buddhism

LOVE

"Love is being there."

—Thich Nhat Hanh

When I began to surrender to tears I noticed a subtle shift in my heart. A presence felt that I had forgotten. Occasionally, when I would notice that I was in my head, I would drop down into my heart and feel a surge of revitalizing energy, it made me feel happy.

Upon contemplating the sensation I realized that I was feeling the energy of love. Something I had thought I had always felt, yet now understood that perhaps I had indeed forgotten how to feel love move through me. I suppose after all these years of not accepting my vulnerability, and denying myself the outlet of crying I should have expected this to happen. I have found that it has been easier to give love than to receive it. Yet, I have now begun to graciously accept love from others, and from within myself for myself.

I can't imagine all of you have, nor will, experience this. Indeed, I suspect many of you know how to love deeply, in both the giving and receiving. You may have simply just found yourselves unable to grieve. Thus, this portion of the book may not speak to you as deeply as it speaks to others. Nevertheless, I feel that it is necessary.

When one dwells in love, your whole being radiates forth a beautiful light. Your eyes are shiny, and there is a stillness within you. If you have never met such a person, I urge you to seek one out. Seek a spiritual teacher, an older martial arts teacher etc… We all need to experience that in another, so that we can accept the potential in ourselves.

So what is Love for me, and how could I have forgotten about it?

My understanding of Love is that it is a form of energy. It existed within us when we were born, and it cannot be turned off via the mind. It is an energy that emanates from every human being when we are in our natural state of peace, dwelling in the realm of compassion.

Of course, love can also be perceived to have many forms. Platonic love, love for a child, love for an activity etc… However, when one surrenders to the feeling of love at its core, these perceived different forms are really artifacts of the power of loving.

Other people may state that love is an emotional response. Based on the above I tend to disagree. There's falling in love. However, that is temporary too. Hence the phrase *"Honeymoon Period."* As you get to know someone over time, your understanding of them may cause you to foster compassion towards them and hopefully visa-versa. If a couple stays committed to each other long enough, there is a moment when you see, and *really* see that person, warts and all. Then you realize that there is an energy between the two of you. You are at peace with each other, accepting. That's when the connection is felt.

There's the idea that you love to do something. That again seems to be referring to an emotional response of happiness. I love to play my guitar, however, when I play my guitar the energy of love flows because I am at peace in that moment. That's what I enjoy, the ability for the instrument to move me out of my head and into my heart.

So how does one know when they feel this energy? I guess it can be similar to when one is asked "*Have you ever been in love?*" If my response was "*I think so*", the questioner knew I hadn't, yet after I had fallen in love for the first time I could only respond with "*Yes, I have.*" There was certainty in my voice, you knew I had then. The same goes for when you have touched the power of real love within yourself. If you can remember back to that time, you may notice that you were at peace with yourself and your environment. You felt charged somehow. Your heart was open; you had a sparkle in your eyes. Many good things happened to you as you attracted more love.

"*But isn't love just another emotion?*" I hear you ask. I'm reminded of a story I read while in India around defining what an emotion is.

Imagine that you are an empty cup in the middle of a circle. Around the circle are other cups each filled with their respective emotion. One cup is the cup of anger, the other of jealousy, another anxiety etc... All are still. You're in your car driving along paying close attention to the road, when the empty gas tank light comes on. You need gas, yet you don't have enough money. Within your mind a thought arises that draws you out of the present moment. You remember that a friend borrowed money and hasn't paid it back, and you associate that with not having enough money to pay for gas. If that emotion is strong, the cup of anger begins to vibrate. The stress of not having enough money causes you to become angrier. As you allow the thoughts to continue you get more and more angry. At this time the cup of anger beings to pour itself into you. The more attention you give the cup of anger the more it continues to pour. Until eventually you are now full of anger. Your mind has allowed an emotion to take over you. You have become angry.

The same happens for other emotions if we are not mindful. Once this is recognized, a person can begin letting go of the emotion and begin to pour back into the cup of anger as they let go. Focusing on the numbers while counting to ten is a common task prescribed in order to calm oneself down.

Thus, for me, an emotion is temporary as it arises within the mind. Again, that is not love as love isn't temporary. You can most certainly amplify the feeling of love with thoughts, or bury it deep within yourself, however it is always present.

How does one let go of emotions then, in order to feel love as much as possible? Well a good exercise is this:

> The next time you have a thought that causes the cup of anger to vibrate, say to yourself "*Look, there's anger again.*" This validates the emotion. Observe the cup vibrating, yet let it go on vibrating. Bringing yourself into the present moment by focusing your attention toward your body. Over time you will sense the energy of anger just before it arises, and instantly remind yourself not to get attached to it. It's ok to feel angry, just don't become attached to it. Eventually, the cup will stop bothering to vibrate, as it knows it won't get any attention. The reason I like this image is that it denotes that I have a choice in how I react to my emotions; they are not who/what I truly am. I am witnessing them.

Actors use the fact that emotional states can be created simply with a thought to conjure truth in their performance. Understanding how to *see* the progression of dialogue for the character allows the actor to seek images that will elicit the correct emotional response during the performance.

Remember to have compassion for yourself if upon doing the exercise you find yourself consumed with anger, that's ok as acknowledging it is the first step towards becoming more aware, more mindful of that emotion.

Moving on, I have observed that the love I cultivate flows when I am in a natural state of peace. "*Well aren't we all mostly in a state of peace?*" In order to really understand that question, you have to contemplate what life was like many, many years ago. Let's not dwell on what a civilized society brings to the game, because let's be honest the advances are offset by the setbacks such as climate change, WMD, GMO, worsening quality of life for some etc... Let us simply contemplate how people co-existed with nature.

Before the agriculture revolution people understood that they were part of a system, they abided by the system's rules, meaning; they didn't consume more than they needed, honored the land and sea in which they utilized. They saw themselves as one of the inhabitants like all the other life forms. For the most part, they did their chores in the morning, and at night. The remaining times they socialized, meditated, contemplated their existence and feeling at one with others and Mother Nature. The stress came when the food ran out, when predators threatened the tribe etc...

Daniel Quinn wrote an interesting book titled *Ishmael: An Adventure of the Mind and Spirit* that discusses this form of existence where indigenous tribes were for the most part very peaceful, and left no trace. I highly recommend you read it as it offers a different point of view on how we in the modern world are evolving, and why.

Today however, we are very rarely at peace. The stress felt by the body of those people in the pre-agricultural days was not continuous, unlike how our existence is today. Therefore, the body had the opportunity to rebalance.

The effect of stress, the fight/flight response, causes the body to release chemicals like adrenaline, noradrenaline and cortisol into our bloodstream. Our body undergoes a dramatic change because we are not at ease, or in a state of disease, if you will. Blood is diverted away from our digestive tract and directed into our muscles and limbs, which consume extra energy and fuel for running and fighting. When I've been stressed for several days, I find myself completely exhausted.

You can see quite clearly, within yourself too, that we modern humans are hardly ever in our natural state of peace. That is we rarely find ourselves without our inner voice chitchatting to us, our nerves settled, enjoying each and every moment to it's fullest. We always seem to be in some level of flight/fight response: stressed out, hormones never given enough time to rebalance before we manifest the next anxious moment. Western people in particular tend to have a hard time sitting still; our minds are overactive due to the enormous amount of stimuli we subject ourselves to. A few people are so unable to stop the inner monologue that they are deemed somewhat insane. I guess to some degree then, we're all leaning towards insanity.

As I stated early, the one thing I noticed over the years was that I had lost the real sense of the feeling of love within myself. No amount of trying to remember that feeling, or thinking back to a time when I knew I was flowing with love would trigger a sense memory bringing me into that state. That's when I began to sense that part of who I was wasn't being properly acknowledged; the vulnerable side. Constantly trying to maintain that I wasn't vulnerable, or didn't need to show my vulnerability (to cry), denied me the element of peace within myself. Thus causing me to build walls around my heart, not allowing the energy of love to come into me, nor from me.

After I had remembered how to cry, and cry hard (due to another heartbreak) that's when I sensed a shift within myself. Being so guarded I failed to fully appreciate life. The tears may have caused a loosing of the bricks within the walls around my heart, allowing me to open up and soften.

I have observed that many have a tendency to only give love to their immediate family and friends. They withhold love towards people in a neighboring town, city, state and even country, all because of the inability to see how we are all connected. Science has now drawn the same conclusions around connectedness that all the major spiritual paths and religions have stated; we ARE all connected. That ourselves and our environment shape us on a cellular level. The emerging field of Epigenetics studies just that.

When I read his Holiness the Dali Lama's book on "*How to expand Love*" the section that was the most influential described how if one believes in reincarnation then at some point in your many times here in the material plane everyone you meet today would have at one time or another been your Father, Mother, Sister, Daughter, Brother, Son, Grandchild, Grandparent etc… Think about that for a moment. If everyone you met may be considered your family, wouldn't that change how you would greet them. Imagine having a day where you demonstrated a little bit of love for every person you met. Imagine the love you'd start to receive.

The tears shed during your exercise may lead to something greater than a simple release. Feeling the energy of love from within you, and without you, gives a deeper purpose to your commitment to remember how to cry.

CULTIVATING LOVE

> "*Love never reduces the other to a thing; on the contrary love raises the other to divinity. Love transforms ordinary human beings into gods.*"
>
> —Osho

The exercises within the section on compassion will lead you to have more kindness towards yourself and others. This in turn will lead you towards a more peaceful existence. From within that peaceful state you may find the energy of love beginning to flow from your heart. As you begin to sense this shift within yourself I would ask that you introduce another morning exercise.

Again looking at yourself in the mirror add to the earlier statements "*I love you*".

Essentially what I'm saying when I say that to myself, is that the love I feel flowing from my heart I gift to you the one I see in the mirror.

If you live alone, additional ways of cultivating love may include introducing something within your environment that requires you to take care of it. e.g. Plants, or fish. Something small rather than a pet, simply because a pet requires more effort, and perhaps you're not in the position to take on such a responsibility.

FEAR/ANXIETY

"He who is not everyday conquering some fear has not learned the secret of life."

—Ralph Waldo Emerson

Fear is a very powerful distressing emotion. Many years ago it was a useful indicator when the flight/fight response really meant either you fought or you took flight because otherwise your survival was in jeopardy. i.e. You would be killed.

Today, fortunately for most people, fight or flight response in the truest sense rarely happens. However, fear is still ever present. Or rather what is now termed anxiety.

You can find a lot of information around fear. Some say it's a sign that your root chakra isn't balanced, or that it's your soul's way of letting you know you're not on your true path. You'll find what may constitute helpful statements such as: *"It's all in your head"* and *"Laugh at fear"*. Echoed by friends, family and teachers. There's so much information it'll make your head explode.

Ah fear.

How did my fear play into denying my vulnerability? Was there a direct moment when my fear caused me to evaluate and change the way my life was progressing? Moving away from allowing my feelings to exist? Well, I would say yes there was, it occurred at a young age.

Like many boys (and these days girls included) locking down my ability to cry was a way to demonstrate that I was not afraid. During a playground fight, not showing tears demonstrated strength, or so I believed. My environment enforced this belief time and time again. Growing up in London, England, one hears a lot of "Boys don't cry", "Stiff upper lip" etc. And without proper mentoring, how could I have deduced an alternative?

As I grew older, and the fear shifted into anxiety, I held tight to that playground belief not really understanding the difference between the two emotions; they sure felt the same. Another side effect was that I was now afraid to cry for fear that I would become too weak to carry on my life with the same strength and courage and that others would lose faith in me, their trust in my ability to be someone they could lean against would be diminished. So I held the fear in, and one day I found that my fear and anxiety began to eat me from inside.

Today, there are many techniques to conquer your fears of flying, heights, death. But what of my fear of crying? How do I conquer that? Well I learned fear isn't to be conquered, it's to be felt deeply then released by coming to terms with what you are afraid of by holding it up to the light, thereby gaining an understanding of why you fear it. Doing something that I feared greatly, crying, gave me that insight. As the saying goes "*Courage is doing that which you fear, yet continue to do despite it.*" This is not an easy thing to do, holding something so powerful up for scrutiny, exposing oneself to such pain. I sought help from friends, I'd advise you to be cautious and seek counsel if the pain becomes to great.

Funny enough simply making a commitment to let go was enough to get me on the right path, accepting that I was afraid and that it was ok to be afraid.

An amazing thing happened the first time I cried, I felt very grounded afterwards. Fear (or anxiety), for the moment, had left me. Especially, the fear of crying.

So? It is ok to feel fear? Everybody at one time or another will feel fear. So you are not alone in that. What is important is that you ask why. Why do I fear not having enough money? Why do I fear never meeting someone to settle down with? Fear of retirement, etc… I found that my fears all came down to the fact that I was vulnerable, and that I had no control over that. The future is uncertain. Could I solve this problem? For me the answer was yes; by accepting my vulnerability. For you at this time, you may find that is a little more difficult. So the answer is "*No, I can't solve the problem at this time.*"

> "*If the problem has a solution, worrying is pointless, in the end the problem will be solved. If the problem has no solution, there is no reason to worry, because it can't be solved.*"
>
> —Zen saying

YIN AND YANG

"No two of the products of creation are alike. From this we know that although the number of things is infinite, at bottom there is nothing without yin or yang. From this we know also that the transformations and changes in the universe are due to these two fundamental forces."

—Chang Tsai

At the time of this writing I'm living in the San Francisco Bay Area due to Silicon Valley being one of the better places to work as a Software Engineer.

Prior to moving here I had spent several years in Sydney, Australia. While there I had been studying Shotokan karate, and Yoshikan Aikido. I was most definitely feeling very grounded, and very masculine. I left because I had ended a relationship that represented my first time of being in love; deeply felt love. And Sydney seemed to be losing it's hold on me, time for a change.

Many years later a friend noted that he had never seen me grieve for the loss of that woman. He was right of course; I had not allowed myself to cry. My reasoning was that I just wasn't able to let go; to fall into my softer self. I was holding onto the idea that I was too old for tears, too much down the path of manhood. It took several years for the truth to be realized, and several encounters with the concept of masculine/feminine energies.

During my time here in the Bay I have observed that there is a lot of feminine energy here, and a common complaint that I hear from women is that there aren't any "*real*" men. Women appear to have a more controlling sense about them, more akin to what I would find in men in other parts of the country. The men here seem softer, more wanting to experience the flow of the world and I suspect this may be due to the number of spiritual paths that can be found here. If I were to ponder the reason why the Bay area has so many such paths, I would have to defer to the Ying/Yang idea of balance. The opposite of a spiritual path would be the pursuit of materialistic riches. Silicon Valley and the "*get rich quick*" dream that accompanied the .COM era would be the obvious counterpoint.

In any event Masculine/Feminine energy is a term used quite often today. What do they mean exactly?

MASCULINE ENERGY

Masculine energy is found to some degree in both of the sexes. It is the energy of purpose, focus, and accomplishment. It is the problem solving, goal setting, driven attributes. This energy is perceived in one who has a sense of purpose, is self-disciplined, moving confidently towards their goals with clarity. It may be considered the harder, more pragmatic side of a person. Feet on the ground. The provider, the protector.

FEMININE ENERGY

Feminine energy is also found to some degree in both of the sexes. It is the energy of being receptive, intuitive, sensitive, emotional, and nurturing. Some would say it is the energy of creation. For without harnessing one's ability to nurture, the creation will die. It may be considered the softer, dreamier side of a person. The gentle healer.

HARMONY

As David Deida notes in his book "*The Way Of The Superior Man: A Spiritual Guide to Mastering the Challenges of Women, Work, and Sexual Desire*" most relationships will have someone who feels and looks like a more masculine person, and a more feminine person. Whether a heterosexual couple, or a gay/lesbian couple, it is easily observed. Even in intimacy someone will be more in their masculine energy, and this can change each time a couple is intimate (and during). i.e. one will choose to be more dominate over the other, they're controlling the flow. With time, as the couples journey together unfolds, the energies can flip-flop rapidly as trust and surrender occur.

Understanding which of the two is dominant in yourself is important, especially as you age and begin to feel a shift within. This can be confusing as men who have never felt afraid, nor vulnerable, may begin to sense emotions more deeply as they age. This is normal, and I would generalize by saying it's because our testosterone level decreases substantially after we hit a certain age (somewhere around 38), thus causing our estrogen level to become proportionately more present which in turn softens the male aggressive tendencies.

Wisdom comes from experience coupled with the compassionate ability to provide nurturing advice to others. Picture a Native American Indian chief on who is strong, gentle, wise and loving. Or a compassionate grandmother.

Mythology teaches us a great deal about how our lives may unfold, unfortunately the term Myth has been compromised to mean false, untrue. Far from it, myths are sacred narratives, stories explaining how our world and we humans came to be. One of the reasons the movie "*Star Wars*" is such a success is that the myth of the Hero's journey portrayed is so well known on a subconscious level, and it is very clear who were the good guys and bad because it was so very black and white.

Myths teach us men that in our younger years we feel the pull of the world on us. We feel the need to explore. We will make mistakes, yet our courage allows us to learn and persist and keep moving forward relishing that desire to experience life. However, at some point a man will feel the need to experience the inner world. The world of the Self. Again generally speaking, Women feel a different pull, the need to experience life from the power of creation via children. To raise a family, reap the rewards of love from their children. However, at some point a woman will also feel the need to experience the inner world.

The point is that both sexes after many years, are depicted as ending up at the same point. They desire to find the meaning of their existence. Awareness has grown within each, and a sense that there's more begins to be felt.

In modern times however, things have changed. The roles of father and mother have become blurred as both sexes took on more of the others responsibilities. In one sense this is a good thing. However, it does create some difficulties in relationships, and it has caused a great deal of confusion for what is acceptable behavior for men especially around our need to cry.

In my opinion it stems from an inability to reconcile the balance of masculine/feminine energies within oneself. A woman who chooses to go into the workforce may lose her feminine self as she attempts to compete with the men by becoming more masculine. Hilary Clinton is a good example of this I would say.

Some men (myself included) being raised by our mothers and not having a father present, nor a clearly defined role model, or most importantly a rite of passage, would have struggled with understanding what being a Man meant. What were the positive traits required? Meeting strong women makes things even more confusing, as banging heads with a woman is considered inappropriate behavior. A gentleman opens the door, never strikes a woman etc...

It's no wonder today many of us feel confused in relationships; sensing something's amiss.

As I stated earlier, in a relationship there is a requirement for the presence of both energies. If a woman is stronger, and the man wishes to be *the man,* a conversation has to occur in order to shift the balance. That conversation will take great courage, and require the deepest trust. To illustrate this more clearly some authors will advocate the need for the woman to surrender to the male sense of purpose and to yield to him by following him on his mission in life.

If you are a woman reading this, and you have been in the workforce doing just fine, you'd probably be resenting that statement. However, let's look at it a different way. At some point in your life you may have felt that having to go to work wasn't exactly what you wanted to do. A sense that the job was taking you away from simply enjoying your children, the people around you, basically causing you to miss out on your life. If you reached this point, you had a few choices. Surrender to your masculine energy, yielding to "*him*" in order to continuing having the opportunity to enjoy your life, or not. You had to find balance and acceptance with the energies within yourself.

Back to Deida's book "*The Way Of The Superior Man: A Spiritual Guide to Mastering the Challenges of Women, Work, and Sexual Desire*". It is aimed at, but not solely for, heterosexual men. It defines attributes of his idea of a superior man, and how a woman determines a superior man. A man in a healthy relationship is driven by purpose, has strength and can be a pillar against which the woman can lean against when needed.

Think back to earlier times when male/female roles were pretty cut and dry. Man was provider and protector; woman gave birth and raised the children. As I said, the balancing of the roles today is a good thing as it allows each to see the world from the others eyes. However, let's not forget that women chose their men based on his ability to provide and protect, even if they consciously may not admit it. Her priority would be the children, and the family. That fundamental perception of how a couple comes together hasn't changed much, even if our understanding or acceptance of it has. What transpires later in life when the family begins to take shape is a different matter as being a house husband is a common life choice nowadays.

Still, today a woman has a tendency to test her man (push buttons if you will) to see his strength. How she does this varies, the overriding purpose however doesn't change. She does so in order to feel safe when surrendering to him.

The term surrender here isn't used as in defeat, it is used to denote a willingness for deeper intimacy. Surrender requires trust, a woman will yield to her man when the man believes in himself and has courage and strength to stay on target in regards to commitments. She will trust him and soften.

The last few paragraphs have allowed me to introduce a point in regards to choosing an appropriate time to cry. There may be times when you have to hold in your pain while those around you let theirs out. If the woman you are with is feeling weak and vulnerable, your job is to be there for her, your time will come to let go. Therefore, I would advise that you be mindful of each situation. Sadness will strike, and through your practice you will feel the stirrings of tears. At such times remember to breath deeply, and quiet your mind. Listen to her intensely, and observe the moment. Make a commitment to yourself to visit your cave so as to release the pain. If possible, especially at a time of grieving, communicate a desire to cry to your partner. Or sit with a friend and let the tears fall. Allowing other men to see your vulnerable side consciously can be very healing. However, be cautious as some women do not want to see their man in tears as it may weaken their faith in his strength.

RITE OF PASSAGE

"I'm only interested in rites of passage stories."
—Pete Townsend

A *rite of passage* is a ritual or ceremonial event that marks a period in time whereby a person moves from one stage of life into another. Most societies have at one time or another recognized the need for such events.

Being raised by my mother (as I'm sure several men my age were) finding adequate role models was difficult. Not having an adult male to turn to for guidance meant a young boy would have to fend for himself in regards to deducing what was considered manliness. Seeing the power of tears in a healthy context may be a powerful life lesson for a young lad to experience. Luckily, I was blessed with a keen power of observation and an intelligence that allowed me to see aspects of human behavior that I felt would be worth incorporating into my own being. Those people included uncles, aunts, teachers, friends of family, family of friends, lovers, movie characters, book characters, etc… I would sense traits that I felt represented a healthy human persona, as well as detecting traits that would be counter-productive to gracefully traversing a lifetime.

The most influential man was my father. He taught me how *not* to be a man. I later realized that he was simply being himself the best he knew how, struggling with life's journey, as we all are. To clarify I felt that his upbringing, his pain, his insecurities and the resulting life path he chose for himself were not inspiring for me. What I saw in him I did not equate to the idea of a warrior/hero that I admired, and decided that that's *not* how I wish to live my life. I did respect the fact that I was his son, and traits within him would certainly exist within me. Over the years moving from boyhood to manhood I made a conscious effort to note any of those traits that manifested (especially the negative ones), and dug deep into my psyche to understand why they existed. Why did I feel that marriage and children were not for me? That I had to follow my own heart, and live my own journey no matter what? How could a man beat the woman he loved? Where were those insecurities coming from?

In respect to abusive behavior, I needed to address this in order to heal from what I had seen as a young child, and to ensure I never fell into such a trap. Over time I began to understand my own dislike of violence along with this repulsion to the idea of engaging in a fight. Meaning that if I were in a situation where someone wanted to fight me, I would not engage. Was this cowardly behavior? Not necessarily, although from an outside perspective it could easily be seen that way. Indeed, for me the idea of hurting another person, letting my anger loose, was the deciding factor. I couldn't do it. I didn't understand how to control that anger and aggression and that's what scared me. I had seen that anger a few times within myself and recognized it to be the same anger my Father unleashed on my mother. Therefore, I would hold it in regardless of the consequences. This lead to my interest in the Martial arts. In these arts I could learn to control the anger and aggressions, harness them in a healthy way. Becoming confident in knowing that I had a choice, and if pushed I could defend myself. Part of the training required that I put on more muscle mass. A friend created a weight training program for me, and I was off and running full steam towards Manhood.

Many years later I realized that I had inadvertently stumbled upon my own *rites of passage*. I had found mentors, teachers, fellow young men that allowed me to create rituals, codes of conduct and markers to which I could gauge as progress into manhood. Even something as simple as bench-pressing 135 lbs was a sort of rite in the weight room.

I sense that western society may have forgotten the importance of the Rites Of Passage for both sexes awaiting the transition into adulthood. The rise of the nuclear family, the "*keep up with the Joneses*" mentality, slowly eroded a sense of community. Or more importantly, the rites we do have such as baptisms, bar mitzvahs and confirmations, school graduation ceremonies, weddings, retirement parties, and funerals seem to lack the necessary weight and guidance from an older generation. They do not adhere to the Mythology of going out into the world and finding yourself. They all lead less towards the warrior and more towards the good employee, soldier. Subordinate; not leader.

I have noticed that without proper ritualized acknowledgment of an important stage of life, we as individuals lose our connection with the greater tribe. We lose our ability to understand the importance of the cycle of life. We forgo an appreciation for those who have come before us, have lived as children, have grown, have faced the same challenges that we will face, and most importantly have dealt with and are preparing for death. In doing so we have lost respect of our elders, and the social structure around authority has diminished to the point of it becoming extinct. We have lost our ability to use our voice in a constructive manner. Without adequate role models within the tribe, we stumble; we do not have an opportunity to recognize our strength and our responsibilities to the greater good of the planet.

I read an interesting article a few years back in the New York Times written by Charles Siebert regarding rogue elephants and the reasoning behind their behavior. A researcher, Gay Bradshaw, had documented that elephants are "*profoundly social creatures*". There is a clearly defined social structure, and wonderful sense of responsibility from each adult within the herd towards the young. The females from all generations—mother, aunts, grandmothers, and friends, raise the young. After eight years the females start the process of being integrated into the matriarchal network, and the young males join the all-male elephants until mature enough to join the adults. Due to the enormous amount of poaching, the adult elephants had dwindled away to very few. Without the elders to keep the young in line the male elephants in particular suffered due in part to their traumatic experiences from viewing the violence of poaching, and not having a supporting environment in which to heal. The result being that normal brain and behavioral development was deeply impaired. Without a sense of boundaries the male elephants became rogue.

This is an extreme case that I'm using to illustrate a point in respect to where we are today. With our culture losing the sense of one community (the Earth community) and lacking elders that maintain a realistic notion that only cooperation, the *it's just us* if you will, and not competition which leads to the "*us and them*" trap that we so often see nowadays, we may not survive as a species. One tribe pitted against the other isn't working, whether it's rich and poor, employer and employees, teachers and students, parents and children, it all manifests into individuals that do not understand that it is "*our planet*", "*our pain*", "*our joy*", "*our success*", "*our failure*", "*our life*", "*our death*". The media loves this; they can sell more ad space. I wonder what would happen if the old tribal ways found their way back into modern society? Would people have less stress, less anxiety? Would we exhibit more compassionate behavior towards each other and ourselves? Would our ability to recognize and utilize the power of crying increase? Perhaps.

A LIFE'S JOURNEY

"Time is the wisest counselor."

—Pericles

Ones life unfolds in ways unexpected, the only thing certain is uncertainty. In the preceding chapters I conveyed some of the more essential lessons, observations and insights that I have accumulated to date. Of course, much of what I have written captures my current understandings of myself and the world in which I move and I fully expect my perceptions to change. Perhaps the information will become more precise as I continue articulating and utilizing the sentiments expressed. In the end, I hope you have related to some of the information, questioned parts and even disagreed with me here and there. At best I trust you are able to peer into your own heart and acknowledge that you feel a need to continue to move forward, yet not in the same manner as before.

Do not underestimate your own strength, when the time comes for you to call upon it you will be surprised at how strong a vulnerable spirit you can be.

Comments and/or questions can be sent to: StrengthWithinTears@gmail.com.